A. T. AND FRIENDS

SPREAD THE GOOD NEWS

A. T. AND FRIENDS

By A. T. Classic

MONARCH TRAILS PUBLICATIONS/DETROIT

DEDICATED
WITH LOVE AND APPRECIATION TO
J II

Library of Congress Catalog Card No. 87-60732
ISBN: 09616665-0-1

PUBLISHED BY
MONARCH TRAILS PUBLICATIONS
P.O. BOX 05272
DETROIT, MICHIGAN 48205

Printed by Harlo Press, 50 Victor, Detroit, Michigan 48203

PREFACE

When a writer puts out his first book, the sense of joy in accomplishment tempts toward pride. But the path which leads to success often humbles and always disciplines. Dues paid up front seem to equate to the dynamic duo of death and taxes.

The desire to know and then to share this knowledge is a divine urge that can seem both a blessing and curse in one. Who do you think you are? What could you have to say that would be worth my time? You ain't nobody. Just a dreamer. Boy, you think you a know-it-all. Ain't you LeRoy's son? Man, you better get a job. Doubts withstanding, I humbly offer this book, a consideration of the issues of life.

Solomon advises, "In all thy getting, get understanding." "A knowledge of The Holy is understanding." I quote my favorite writer and now add my own musing upon his thought. Understanding comes as information is cognized, then recognized, enabling one to make profitable decisions.

Musing is the term I choose as best defines my approach to writing. Sometimes I think it's amusing. As a muse-ition, I take poetic license to be creative with language. In the Golden Age of Greece, Muse was the goddess of inspiration for poets. As you will see, much of my writing is in a poetic style and will best be appreciated as poetic expressions of my perceptions.

Contained within this body of work are writings of friends. Their initials follow their work. Special thanks to Uncle Harry.

—A. T. Classic

CONTENTS

Awareness

FRIEND

friend (frend) n. 1 One who cherishes kind regard for another person; an intimate and trustworthy companion. 2. One who is committed to another's aid by agreed ally relationships.

Teachers are friends,
Least ways the best ones are.
Friend to boys and girls:
A Blessed Way to Live.
Guiding tiny feet;
Opening hungry minds.

I Love Teachers. Teachers I Love. The best friend and Master Teacher is Jesus. His gift is shared through many. Misses Herbert, Hanks, Jones, Brown, Clark, Coleman, Cobb, McDaniel, Robinson. Misters White, Hamlin, Brown, James, Meeks, Harrington, Ames, Williams, and the Man who hired all these people, Mr. Henry Fortson. Bless You All.

—A. T.

PALMER PARK

Searchin
Searchin
Seeking
Seeking
Searchin
Looking
Over
Under
Between
Between
Beneath
Below
Always on the Lookout

For those who want to know

ONLY THE BLESSED

I've discovered a life secret!!
EVERYTHING IS IN IMAGINATION!!!
Where I go from here is up to me.

The dung of life has blessings
That only the Blessed see.

LOVE ON THE WING

The flight of a Monarch catches my eye
Beauty in motion elicits a sigh
Clearly he shows us by fluttering wing
God is our Father Love is His Thing
On the scent of a rose he flutters away
Adrift on the wind in papillion play
Thank you Father for giving me sight
I delight in watching the Monarch in flight
In tune with each heart who's sigh is a hail
Praise to the Father lifts to the sky
Each time I see a Monarch pass by

BRAND NEW ME

When life in you is
It's not by your command
Your next breath just may not be
So skip the lie about a tree
Living by the law of God
Is light to the blinded man
Six days did He labor
In the seventh is a hallowed plan
Remember thou art created
This rule doth set you free
God First in everything
God First in thee
Walking the path of His understanding
I'm Born The Brand New Me

MAY THIRD

Well I never
In all my born days
Happy birthday world
The Son whose son thou art
Returneth to set you free
No longer live in doubt
Of His presence in thee
Believing is seeing
His kingdom doth live in we

WANNA BE

I wanna ah be ah writer in the worstest kinda way
Ah spends all my time reading
And Ah knows what ole massas say
I wants ti be a writer wif something sound fa today
Drawing memories of tomorrow looking back at
yesterday
I want to be a writer in the most deserving way
Crystalize the spoken dream of His soon returning
day
I want to be a writer and write the spoken word
"He stepped out in space and spoke us from his
grace
Now we standed redeemed of that lost and fallen
race"
I want to write a picture of his never failing grace
Perfect made he perfect   The only way to be
Living in His will is always best for thee
Doing my own thing   is   Doing my own thing
Not The Father's Way to See
I want to write a picture of the Love he spent for we
Tells us God is Father Man's not descendent from the
sea
Love is God's motive   Forever we were meant to be
Picture   Picture   on my mind
Love Begat Love   Kind Begat Kind
Fruit of the Father   Brother of the Son
Redeemed of His Spirit   The One and Holy One
Oh comforter and Guide to truth that sets me free
I want to be a writer of human history
In the beginning was The Word   And The Word is
He

Beginnings

HISTORY OF THE PLANET EARTH

According to the Bible the earth was created. Psalms 33:6-9 says God spoke the world into existence. Man was created with Adam and Eve as the first human beings. Adam lived nine hundred and thirty years (930). Adam begat Seth when he was a hundred thirty. Seth lived nine hundred twelve years. In his one hundred fifth year he begat Enos. Enos begat Cainan in his ninetieth year and lived all together eight hundred fifteen years. He begat Mahalaleel in his seventieth year. And all the years of Mahalaleel were eight hundred ninety five. In his sixty fifth year he begat Jared. Jared lived a hundred sixty two years and begat Enoch. All the years of Jared were nine hundred sixty two. Enoch lived sixty five years and begat Methuselah. All the days of Enoch were three hundred and sixty years and God took him alive to eternal life, Methuselah lived (969) years and begat Lamech in his one hundred eighty seventh year. Lamech begat Noah in his hundred eighty second year. All the years of Lamech were (777). And Noah lived five hundred years and begat three sons, Ham, Shem and Japheth. All the begats and overlapping times total approximately two thousand (2000) until Noah. After Noah, 14 generations lead to David King of Israel. From David until Jesus of Nazareth is another fourteen generations. All together from Adam to Jesus was forty two generations of man, totaling four thousand years. A thousand nine hundred eighty seven leaves us just thirteen years from six thousand years old.

I SEE GOD IN EVERYTHING

God imprints all creation
Each life given birth
Is to His adoration
The flight of a Monarch
Nectar of a Bee
Pattern of a Peacock
Blooming of a Tree
I see God in everything
And am most amazed
When I see God in Me

THE FATHER KNOWS

It all depends on how you see
Cause what it is is up to thee
Imagination makes it so
All you do is let it flow
Up is down when you're blown away
Too Too High you just can't stay
Down is up to those who know
This dip is just part of the flow
Same thing makes you happy makes you blue
What you get is what you do
See your thought in His control
He knows what's coming with the roll
Let it roll let it roll let it roll

KEEP THE FAITH

Difficulties come upon us
As blessings for tomorrow
Down it plops and the dung has stung
Smells of ill foul a rose scented day
Flat tire   loose wire
Frustration run 'a muk'
Day that makes you shout "Oh Suck"
Wink an eye to see time fly
The darkest hour soon passes by
Thou the midnight tareman
Sows your field
The deed won't pass the miller's wheel
Keep your faith and praise His name
He turned the dung into tomorrow's grain
Blessings in the sunshine
Blessings in the rain
What ever comes upon Me
Me Lord can turn to gain

BEHOLD EQUALS CHANGE

Little by Little   Drop by Drop
Water wears out steel
Idea by Idea Thought by Thought
The Person I become
Is the vision I have wrought
Lying in a bed conceiving our own will
Lust heaps upon lust as our cup reaches fill
Gazing into ungodliness
Claiming such is light
Slipping into darkness
An everlasting night
Remember:
Thought wears out flesh
Like water wears out steel
So constantly Behold Him
To Walk in The Father's Will

A.T. II
A FREE SPIRIT BOUND
IN A NATURE OF FLESH

Sure you are a free spirit
I Am is your only limitation
You can be any animal that you see
From Your eyes a pig could be hip to thee
Learn the fullness of your spirit
As bound by flesh is dangerous you see
'specially where you pee
Don't just find pleasure
With jewels of the family tree
They are not to be squandered
Neither shared with the swine
All pearls passed on
Have potential son
You know you represent mine
Pearls link with The Father's history
Be A Free Spirit
Live within thy fullness being thee
Flesh and blood surround you
It doth hinder thee
Bring it into subjection

It can aid you as well
In the game of life, trading off the family jewels
Is where some folks love to dwell
Don't just play there, be serious as can be
'specially when you aim your pee
Bad aim misleads folk
To a life of wholly hell
Only trade off where your God
Would please to stay a spell
Know the nature of your flesh
Can be an enemy as well
Yield not to every urge
To pass on some history
Some folk only use it
To keep you from being free
Know the Father's history
To Live within the now
Life is not just pain and pleasure
Let's all try out Mary Jane
She might look just like a sister
Even have a strange sounding name
Don't just pass on the family jewels
Cause her husband is away
They are not given to a little boy
Just to find a place to play
Learn that flesh is to be subjected
To the Spirit that knows the inward
dwelling thee
Know the fullness of thy spirit
It can help you live within the now
Being as a boy child is s'pose to be
Flesh and blood
Only transport the free spirit
As it views hell
Moving toward eternity
God has called you His sheep
But you can be
Any animal you want to be

CHARIOTS OF DESIRE

Hey there in your chariot
Cruise control set to stay
Laid back til you get there
Save your energy for play

Chariots of desire
Modern man at play
Wheeling through today's concerns
No thought of yesterday
Give me mine now
Is creed from ancient times

A prodigal arrived in town
Just the other day
Driving his chariot of desire
He could not wait to play
Before long he took the path
That left his life for hire
Smooth and fast is made the way
That leads one to the fire
A money green limousine
Sped him to the top
Indulged in all his heart's desire
Before a sudden drop

Designer wheels speed to low way deals
Made to show an outer glow
That says I'm someone to know
Look at me   I do
Mark Seville Sedan Deville
I am someone behind this wheel
Expensive price the vain do pay
To be the self indulgent
Of the last time day

CELEBRATE

I live in the land of celebration
A place known as the Home of Love
Living life in Gratitude
For all from up above
The Kingdom of heaven is within
I heard the Master say
Invite Him to be your guide
He's with you night and day
I just want to celebrate
A Holy way of livin
I just want to celebrate
I've got Love for Givin

SYDNEY

Reasons and Seasons
The souls that we know
Into our lives
Then
They must go
Purpose is known
As time passes by
The burdens I bare
Strengthen my mind
While this is happening
It doesn't seem kind
Mother and Father
Brother and Sister
All go their way
Seasons be gone
Reasons do stay
The love they shared
Lightens my day
I Miss them
And wish them
God's speed as they go
Each has his path
All have their flow
Name it and claim it
We all like to play
Tomorrows not given
To be yesterday
Live in the season
Called Now or Today
Who knows what the future brings
Can it really matter about yesterday.
Live in the Now
To walk in His way
Fish when it's time
Then
Go and play

SHO NUF RAINED

Didn't it Raiaan
Naw! Man
That was a cloud burst
A flood is what it was
Down pour filled to over flow
Water Water Everywhere
No place else to go
Water Water Water
Thunders Roll
Lightnings Flash
Slosh is the Crash
Of wind blown trees
Driving Frightened Losers
To Their Knees
Yeah! It Sho Nuf Raiaaned

THE FLOOD IS COMING

The flood is coming an we're not in the boat
Living lives as if we're made to float
Vine is laden with fruit that is golden
For time which we live to Him we're beholden
Word from the past has now come to bloom
We soon meet our maker and must be in tune
The best of life is promised you
Keep the covenant of the faithful Jew
The barns bulge with ready ripe goods
Fear follows hunger through the neighborhood
The time time is at its end
Yesterday is when fini begin
We know of a coming promised wind
Hold back! Hold back! The righteous cry
Multiplied millions must not die
Lost in a sea of man made despair
Crying for the Light line from
They know not where
If you think you're sheep
But behave like a goat
The Flood is coming an you're not in the boat
When God's not made the trusted float
The Flood is coming and we're not in the boat
Faith is the life line by which we pray

from the rain filled day
fe upon which we stand
f the savior man
ul the lost in
He just can't win
hen it's up to you
nd is long overdue
ow and storms will rage
to hide in the coming age
Noah preached the gospel truth
Next Flood flames burst through the roof
Flood shaped the land once before
Now mountains skip and thunders roar
Out of the boat in so great a time
Not in His will as we sink in life's rhyme
It happened before and won't happen again
Latter day happenings turn friend against friend
Next time by fire the poets say
No place to hide on a flame filled day
So great a swell of unbridled sin
Resisting obedience forsaking His win
Not hearing the cry salvation is free
By doing His will and bending your knee
While hedonist reign
They seek a new sin
To get a 'new thrill'
While all has been done
And and is over the hill
The time for time
Has come to its end
A pleasure seeker
Is not your best friend
The cares of this world
Are laden with woe
Put God in your life
To give it some go
Trust and Obey
The salvation way

A. T. MUSINGS

The happiest moments in my life
Have been in contemplation of the
Presence of His Spirit in men.
Nothing about a being is of
Greater significance than that
He is loved by God.
Even those that have lost their way
Are still loved by the Father.
How can one, committed to lower values,
Know the fullness of His ways?
God desires we know Him
Through an inner relationship.
Socrates has said, "The unexamined life
Is not worth living."
I say the spirit that lives
According to the flesh is the unexamined life.
You know when I like me the best?
When I catch me having a good thought.
Unless you see the butterfly in you
You lose the gift of nature's example.

A. T. MUSINGS

The view of life as seen by God
Knows every path the mind doth trod.
Try as we may to shift the blame
The sin we sin is ours to claim.
The Devil made me do it
Won't play come judgment day.
Righteous Judgment weighs every motive.
To determine the Real intent
Weighed in the All Seeing Eye
The tongue whose speech is forked to sly.
And after all is said and done
God is Just, All man is One.
Jesus is the Light of Man
His blood cleanseth sin.
He paid the price no man could pay
The perfect life as sacrifice
Redeems on Judgment Day.

THE COST

Pay the price of belief
Take Him at his word.
Taste and know the Bread of Life
Is better than you heard.
Ho! Everyone who is a thirst
Quench the urge to live your worst.
Sup upon His will. Live the Golden Rule.
God first in every all
Redeems the biggest fool.

THE SEED OF BELIEF

A space buried deep within my being
Awaits a seed which can only be planted by me.
A space to be filled by the seed of belief
Once you said believe in Me, I Am Truth and Light.
But being used to seeing as the blind,
I thought I could depend on my own sight.
Now I find I must do what you say.
My understanding is short.
I must cry, help thou my unbelief.
A sign is no longer needed for I feel you Lord,
In Me.
But me is wrapped up in false hiss-tory.
Clear my mind to see as you would have me see.
I believe You shall be found in me, but I am lonely
Waiting on living as only unto thee.
Not knowing who I am
Has kept me from believing in you.
Jesus called us brothers.
He is the way to know God as Father.
He it is that fills the space
Left vacant to believe in Him.

QUESTIONS CAME TO ME

Do I get a chance
To be one who has
met The Son?
Will I know His Voice
Among all the pleasing answers
To my soul searching questions?
Can I be in touch with God
By Repetition?
Mantra
Mantra
The one that comes from
The Redeemer in all eternity.
Let Me know your voice
As within it pleads,
"Take up Thy Cross
And Follow Me."

THE READER

Think
Thought
Mull
Muse
Cognize
What you Choose
When you finish
With your thought
About a friend
Can The Reader
Of your Heart say Amen

MASTER

How do I love Thee?
Let Me Count The Ways.
In all the things I do in life
I've learned to give you praise.
First I'm thankful
You chose to express yourself
Through me.
Now
All the things
I saw in haze
I've learned
To check it
By Your gaze.

HE SAID SHE SAID

He did
She was
If it wasn't for them
They
If
Dit ah peer in the light.
Exile those with excuses
To everlasting night.
He said She said
And the buck never stops here
Project it ain't my fault.
His eye is on a sparrow
And knows my every thought.
Fess up
Come clean
It ain't no use to hide
We all need the Master's Blood
Without it
You just can't slide

CHECKING IT OUT

Today
I've been tripping
Around in the mind of poets.
Poets of many kind
Fast funky rhythm
set
To the mellowest of rhyme.
Confession of the vision seen
First Clear   Then
Through the color of wine.
All Too few recover
From the snakes mean wicked bite,
A cozy way to blind one's self
To the everlasting night.
Lying in the gutter
Is a close dear friend of mine.
Left there by the king of snakes
From the sweet dry bitter vine.
Took him on away from here
Before he's Thirty nine.

"Since drinking is my thing
I require the best."
That's the kind of thought
That laid him to his rest.
Poets
Of a higher plane
May flash the truth to you

It only comes out
As what you already knew.

I miss you Freddy.
I miss you Charlie.
When we were teens
We had such dreams
Now I know why I wouldn't
Drink with you.
I hate what people do
To themselves with alcohol.

SAME THING MAKES YOU LAUGH

Same thing makes you laugh makes you cry.
Same thing makes you live can make you die.
Same thing brings you joy brings you sorrow.
Same thing brings tonight brings tomorrow.
So put those cigarettes down
Before you leave here with a frown.
No more puffing come from you
As you face up to morning dew.
Diggs will wipe away that frown
As he lays you in the ground.
Same thing makes you happy makes you sad
Things we think are good turn out bad.
Things that seem a bummer make you glad.
Though your lung is black on black
And that cough is now a hack,
And your Kool is far from mild.
To him that overcometh
You can still be called His child.

PRAYER OF A SINNER

Dear Lord!
I need help. I need it bad.
The help I need is in my mind, yet
I seem to be tied to my fleshly vices.
Vices are of the flesh and soulful lusting
Makes it sin and I know not to follow
After such thought. Yet Oh! Lord, I fail
To allow myself to be led by thy Spirit.
Help me to be able to completely submit,
Led by your Spirit. I know it is my fault
For willfully following after the baseness
Of my nature, forgive me and set me free
To be what you want me to be.
Humbly yours,
A. T.

LISTEN

LISTEN
With
Your Third Eye
HEAR
Wisdom Of Your
Inner Visions

II CHRONICLES 16:9

I've got my eye on you
I know just what you do
Try as you may to escape my eye
I know when you cry, I hear you sigh
Intimate is my piercing sight
I know your thought
In the darkest tight
You turn to that someone up in the sky
Long enough to get you by
Living your will, doin your thing,
Soon you forget to live his way.
The sure approach to hard times day
I know when you're distressed
I know you when you're wroth
I know you by your pattern
I laid out your cloth

EVERYBODY'S EVERY THOUGHT

Everybody's every thought is all known to thee.
From where you are beyond yonder.
The All knowing See.
In our space of tinyness
We surely seem lost in America's Mess.
Oppression, Regression, Concession,
Deflation, Inflation, Depression,
Restriction, Affliction, Addiction,
Worker, Knave, Slave.
But from beyond an open sky
He sees the tearing of an eye.
Hears each longing before we sigh.
In tune with man from inside out.
In Love with man beyond a doubt.
Knows man's every innerness,
Grants his heart's desire.
Rescue me from poverty,
It leaves my life for hire.
Freedom from the overseer man
Has been our constant plea.
Now we see you set the stage
To make your children free.
No more boss to crack the whip
To drive man to his grave
Tis the spoken will of God
No man should be slave

THERE IS A LION IN THE STREET

Go not on to the world's trails.
It has unbelievable pot holes
Designed to make man fail.
Stay out of the street
If you want to survive.
There is a lion in the street,
Eating people alive.
A roaring lion seeking whom he might kill,
His favorite morsel, the lamb as child
Who lives in God's will.
Go not on the path of the backsliding goat.
A lion is ready to slash your throat.
Temptation is strong to hang in the street.
Those who do become lion's meat.
Love not the world or its devices.
A lion's in the street taking sacrifices.
Drugs and lust and selfishness
Begin this path of woe.
Before you finish with your stroll,
A lion in the street will steal your soul.
Give in to His Spirit to walk in God's ways
He guides us thru danger tho our mind's in a haze.

Love

KAAREN

Twice time seven
Is our first gift from heaven
Thank you for your spirit
Shared among us these fourteen years
One who brightens
Clouds of darkened times
With gentle glowing ways
May your birthday be joyous
Through all the coming days

FRIEND

Friend: He calls me.
Tho-we call me friend,
Then tell me you want me
To go to bed with you
Hah! just using friendship,
No Love? Claiming my body
In friendly terms cheapens me.
Don't you know love me only
Or love me no.

I love my friends
Some more lovingly.

FALLING IN LOVE

When we meet as men and women
Open our hearts to the knowledge
That beyond our longing
For one another
Is a longing for you
And that we can only belong fully
To one another
As we first
Belong to you

TEMPERATE

Normally I am a temperate me
Never too much of any thing
Right up the middle
Not too fast not too slow
Practice my whoa before my go
Speak before I'm spoken to
Never before thinking
Just an even right on the mark
Footprint in the sands of time
Ohpps! You come into sight
I lose my cool
As my throat begins to lump
Heat that makes me stir
Chills that sweat out bumps
Love sure is good for the circulation

THE SUBJECT IS ROSES

The subject is roses
The look is your eyes
The flight is the monarch
The high is the skies
All in All
Is seen in your glance
Love Roses Joy and Romance
A rose by any other name
Could only remind me of you

MONTEREY

Embracing in a field of butterflies
The two of us are one
One with oneness in our eyes
As the honeymoon's begun
Here we are in Carmel
The Monarch graces this dome
He leads to trails of familiar dreams
As it's here we build our home
Butterflies vibrate in love
A message crystal clear
Living by God's design
Is how He brought us here

J II

HEY, YOU OUGHT KNOW
You make my insides glow.
I close my eyes to see by inner sight.
The spirit in you is the spirit in me
One with one equals three.
By faith is seen a sightless spark.
A glow of love dispells the dark.
The sparkle in your eye
A reflection of the inner guy.
One and one do equal three
For when two gather there will I be.
He, The Spirit, loves with glee
When the sparkle in your eye
Looks with love on me.

A MOMENT

Someone I love
Loved me today!
Joy
That thrills my soul
Oh! Moment that lasts all day
Taken in so completely
Filling every emptiness
Leaving room for play
Love so greatly needed
Came to me this day
Happy to smell a rose
Follow a butterfly at play
Praise His name
With the setting of the sun
Feel His Love about me
Thou the darkness has begun
Moment that shares everything
Oh crystal set in time
Uplifting rhythm perfect rhyme
Seen in your glance
That says I'm yours
Be Mine

LOVE SETS ME FREE

Love:
Joy that lights the eye
Graceful you passing by
Lucious Lips
Gorgeous thighs
Breast
That makes my temperature rise
Smile so warm
Spirit so bright
Lifting my soul
To higher flight
Soaring thru tomorrows due
Filling my thought with only you
Tender touch upon my back
Embrace to still my wandering soul
Thank you for your loving hold

THE VESSEL

Love oh love oh love
That sets me free
I thank you for the vessel
Whose form is known as she

Love is
The everlasting agreement
Between souls
Not to disagree
Between loves
Never Starting
Never ending
Always everlasting
Forever blending

BEVERLY

Being in love is my favorite thing
The day you took my hand
Baby girl
Superstar favorite sweetheart
Is who you are
Some are even heard to say
I think I'll call her Boo Bene'
Soul to soul I see us be
"Daddy, look at those butterflies
In that tree."
First there was one
Now we are two
We came to praise Him
Our brother's a Jew
I love seeing you
In me

LIGHT FROM WITHIN

We know
Where we
Are going
We have
Found our way
In the dark
Guided
By a light
From within

GROW OLD
ALONG WITH ME

Grow old along with me
The best is yet to be
The stuff of life
Becomes old hat
When you've been there
Is where you're at
Around around around again
Seasons flow to seasons end
I know what's next
Is what's been before
Seems there's no thing new
Behind any door
It goes around to come around
Till you get the lesson for you
Then higher heights
For greater sights
We can live in a land
Where there are no nights
Begin a journey new
It always keeps me fresh
Seeing life with you

MISSING YOU

I desiderate
At the thought of you
Especially when
I have to wash clothes.
Also
Just when it's too quiet,
Your soft soothing voice
When covered
By many absent days
Seems
Just what is needed

SMALL BLESSINGS

Most of the time
We do not know
When seemingly
Insignificant moments
Are momentous occasions
Praise God for
"Small" blessings

Politics, Racism and Religion

ONCE

I only saw him once
But he passed
From the window
Of my life
I loved
That I saw him
Once
Douglas MacArthur
Omar Bradley
Paul Robeson
Nat King Cole, Jr.
Martin Luther King, Jr.

DE-MOCK-RACIST

desiderate (di•sid'a•rat) v.t. A want felt
Feel the lack of. A country in need of
Statesmenship often sacrifices its young
On the alter of macho brinksmanship.

Whom do these people be?
They live their lives by bigotry.
What a waste of blessed time
Live out their lives
Not know God's rhyme.

democracyst (de•mock•racist) noun,
One who espouses Jeffersonian (Draconian)
Conservatism (Rich get Richer, Poor
Get the shaft). One nation under the god
Money, with some justice for some rich.
Synonym, apartheid, dixie rat, republican
Reagan loyalist, conservative Americanist.

THOUGHTS ON THE ELECTION

The legacy of freedom
Is given us by God
The election of Ronnie Raygun
Shall in no wise reverse
The pendulum of God's movement
For the freedom of his children

11-7-80

SHAME SHAME SHAME

Shame
Shame
Shame on you
Boast to the world
You're a Jew
Delight in showing
David's Sign
Symbol of God's
Chosen
Is your line
You ought to be shame
Do what you did
Yet claim His name
Child of the Father
You take His name in vain
When you treat your brother
Like he is game
Shame
Shame
SHAME ON YOU
I don't believe you are

Jehovah's **E**ternal **W**itness

COSMETIC

Know the nature of the beast
Who's behind that Hollywood smile?
See the lost, its poverty's child.
Words and words that tell a lie,
We'll help the poor. Buy this bye.
Time and time and time again,
Hiss-tory is played to history's end.
Step on the down to reach the top,
When the beast as lamb this role can stop.
Wave the fur that speaks of peace.
Behind cosmetic is raging beast.

SHAME ON YOU

Around the world they call you Jew
Set in place by the red white and blue
Dog your brothers with your steel grey oohzi
Strike at 'terrorist' where ever you choozy
Palestine of Olden days
Begin and Reagan attempt to raze
Child of Jehovah is boastful of you to say
You will have to face His Emissary
The coming judgment day
Known by His actions, Loves His only way
Proud of a kinship that reflects a brighter light
You set His name to shame
Declaring a need to start a fight
Brothers all around you who know not the Father's
name
Allah thou they call Him, you can't treat'um like
game
How dare you call yourself The Eternal Father's child
Raising Hell in Jehovah's name shows your way as
guile
Hypocrits is who you be
When Genocide is what you do,
And I just can't accept you as The Jew

ANY HISTORIAN WILL ATTEST

As any historian will attest, great empires have failed to perpetuate themselves by deterioration from within. The infra structure including the moral fiber of America is its purpose for being. When this character is destroyed, we are no longer what made us a nation of value. Progress toward greater and greater general welfare improvement necessitates laws which promote justice and opportunity for all its citizens. Anything differing from the goal of the constitution meets the stated goals of our enemies.

STATE OF THE UNION

Viewed from my seat in a window
By the road of life
Is a Great and Awful scene
Men on white horses
Charge evil courses
Plotted by Business King
Denying the dignity of man
An Anglo business creed
The poor we shall see
Stand in line to meet his need
The plight of man goes on still
But white against right is not God's will
What goes around comes around
The walls of Babylon fell
Mighty Eagle flying High
Forgets the rules of the sky
Heady at the top heavy on the bottom
Forget the people's plight
Move the country to the right
Kingdoms came and left the stage
Unmet need builds to rage
In darkness is the plotting done
To keep the minds from being one
Destroying the literacy of generations
While we build the biggest bomb
Where there is no knowing the mind is blind
The union becomes connected by darkness
The 'strength' of the country is thusly
Depended upon keeping an ever increasing
class of illiterates subdued. This is an

Inner union weakness which destroys the
Purpose of government. The preamble indicates
The purpose of government is to operate
For the welfare of the citizens. Policies
put into practice which limit educational
Opportunity, job, health and other
Inalienable rights, accomplish what we
Say we don't want our enemies to do to us.
Any policy that destroys educational
Essentials leaving an ever increasing
body of illiterates should be considered
Treasonous. A vision that is too small to
See justice as everyone's right surely
is not in agreement with constitutional purposes of
American government. To plan cuts in the
Just essentials for an ever increasing
Class of consumers is like an act of war
On the people afflicted.
Children and children's children doomed
To less than dignified conditions through
Their whole lives like slaves. To enslave
Forty million Americans should be treasonous.
No consideration of the state of the union
Is complete unless it includes a clear
Understanding of results of policies on the
Welfare of the people. We are seeing the type
Of deregulated practices which destroy
The good for which America should be standing.
What if America has to answer to God for its
Stewardship of the disadvantaged? Will behind
The scenes quiet, ineffective diplomacy
With Apartheid justify Government and Business
Profits at the expense of miseducating a whole
Class of people? The state of the union is
A repeat of ancient cultural patterns which
Develop at the final stages of ruin. I believe
America is being weighed in the balance and
Found wanting.

UP TO MY KEISTER IN SPHINCTERS

Up to my keister in sphincters, scandalous is the sight,
Wide mouth killer sharks are circling to bite.
Questions by reporters being asked in gleeful delight.
Rumble rumble in my gut this is a warning for my butt.
Dealing with the devil is a dangerous game to play.
Offers you a deal that will make your day.
Top of the world, livin first class.
Worry about the future when you forget the past.
Break the laws sworn to uphold, dealing from the bottom
As you stockpile gold. No more a safe haven is our land,
When arms for terrorist is our plan. "Iranian nation
Shall rise some day, I'll give ole Khomeni a backdoor play."
Sphincter sphincter hold in place, keep this top secret,
Pass no waste. Uh oh! Better call image control. My sphincter
Let blow in a public place, I'm a teflon president but
Smell a disgrace. Better that an admiral bust a gut, and go
Into shame, than commander and chief take this blame.
Scapegoat scapegoat you should know. This is the way the

Plan does flow. Machiavelli's concept of the past, deal
With the Devil, cover your ••— (dot-dot-dash)
Up to my kiester in sphincters, yeah, yeah, that's what
I'll tell the press. Toss sphincters to the sharks, they
Serve at my behest. Maybe they'll buy it just to put this
Scandal to rest. Nixon, Kissinger and a group from
the past,
Played loose with our laws and we hoped they'd be
the last.
Re-gun, Raygun, Ambush and the boys, pulling strings
From the same old toys.
Some tried to tell us; but America's will is to not see,
Arrogance and greed is Republican legacy. It seems
all this
Time, some of us knew, Reagan and the boys are the
same old crew.

KNOW A DEVIL WHEN YOU HEAR ONE

How little we know
When we know not The Lord
The thoughts we live
Behind which we hide
Can all be found in T.V. guide
To walk in this world
Not guided by faith
Is Running Blind
In a sighted man's race
Remember the brother
Who lives with no eyes
His ear is his picture
Of the sighted man's lies
He sees just as clear
When ugly is around
The ways of a devil
Come out in his sound
The hiss of his way
By the slit of his tongue
Is heard in the mind of a
Faithful one
Living by sound reveals a strange hum
The lies of the devil don't always seem dumb.
No matter how sweet
The message is sung
The hiss of a devil
is built in his tongue
Tune your sight
To the Inner Man
See by Faith
Know God's Plan

BANTU EDUCATION

Little Black Sambo
Nothing like Rambo
Childhood hero of mine.
I met him in a book
Written by a snook,
To make my people
The laughed at kind.
With a tiger by the tail
That he can't let go,
Around in a circle
In a deep deep rut
To ever slow down
Is a bite out the butt.
Funny to the fool
Who rejects the truth
The boy in the picture
Is a white man's spoof.
In my mind I saw it be
Little Black Sambo is set Free.
A humane twist to this evil plot
Sambo slows his tiger to a trot.
By shoving the tail up his rump
He turned the tiger into a butter lump.
The lies men tell from a biased sight
Do not hold water and can't stand light.

A. T. MUSINGS

The people are blinded by
The realities of what has
Projected them into life.
I was born a __________
Unable to see because
No innate references allow
Re-cognition of what is truth.
People must read The Word
To know.

The forces of nature
Move to bring about God's Will.
When time runs out,
These same forces
Work to annihilate.
I love the ninety first Psalm.
He that dwelleth in the secret
Place of the Most High
Shall abide under the shadow
Of the Almighty.

UNCLE SAM 41

America the beautiful
The way it seemed to me.
Uncle Sam, Protector Man
Defender of what's free.
Keeper of the way of life
Defined DA-Mock-Racy.
Uncle Sam-Defender Man
Bastion of Liberty.
Built this land
On the back of man
He denied dignity.
Opulent
With his ill gained bucks
Entrepreneur in slavery.
Last century
The great white father
That spoke with forked tongue.
A-part-hide on reservations
When genocides begun.

AMERIKA AND AFRIKA

apartheid (a•part•hite) n. S. Afrikann
Word meaning belief of Blacks as
Sub-humans whose purpose is to be
Slaves for the benefit
Of white supremist. It is the
Aryan religious doctrine used to
Dupe whites into practicing
Racial Bias.

MUSING ABOUT
A-part-they-id
Man's id gone wild
Apartheid is CORPORATE
SPONSORED SLAVERY.
Outsourcing = Slavery
American business profits up
Thru Foreign Slavery.
Remove the shame from
American profits, pay
Just wages, world wide.
Evil engages Evil
To profit from another.
America and Afrika
Killing off our brother.

APARTHIED IS

Apartheid is D evil ish
Evil practiced against man.
A sophistry which is hiss-tory.
Tell the slaves his people
Are not supposed to be let go.
His land is yours cause
This is where diamonds grow.
You've got guns and use them too.
Long as no one cares
What gruesome things you do.
You can be Marque DeSau,
Machiavelli too.
Run your guile to hype the world
As you claim to be a Jew.
Keep a slave by whatever name
And shame covers you.
Diamonds of Africa
Reflect its people's soul.
Look past the color
And know the Spirit's goal.
What a shame to invest in land
But never find diamonds in a man.
Evil people just don't care
A brother's soul can go to hell
Long as profits continue to swell.
Apartheid is antibellum at its worse
Reagan is the spokesman
Business is the purse.

Apartheid-Jim Crow-What's in a name
Republican-Dixie-crat-communication game.
Call it what you will, results the same,
Rob a man of his soul all for capital gain.
Evil by what ever name
Is still the work of the devil's game.
Apart from the bigot.
Sleep not with the dog.
Eat not of the swine.
If you don't know why
You must be out of your mind.

GLAD YOU'RE GONE
YOU RASCAL YOU

Same thing that makes you laugh
Can make you cry.
Hand that shakes you hi
Waves good-bye.
Passing bills to rip the poor
Next election you exit the door.
Laugh while you may
Every dog has his day.

DOCKED AGAIN

Why should time be so demanding
When these things are all in vain
Those who work and work and work
I question if they're sane
They who knuckle under to the man
Do his bidding if they can
In on time to punch a clock
Live their lives a boss man's flock
Make him rich as they stay poor
Boss man's cry give me more more more
Times get tough you're out the door
It's all for pense to meet life's need
The boss gets bossy and shows his greed
What a shame to treat man so
Keep him always on the go
Request a raise, NO!
Dock him for his tardiness
Send him home for proper dress
Work him till the sun is down
Give him his pay, call him a clown
How can wages pay for a life
Made to bare the overseer's strife
Time is time to every man
With one life to live
Be the best you can
Respect each life
For soon tis so
We all meet our Master
And Him we must know
Do unto others
As you would have done
Serve the Lord
Love His Son

POLITICIZED WORDS

Terms used to perpetuate the status quo.
Words used in such a way as to keep control
Of peoples along traditional molds.
RACISM: Such a term is a misnomer but
Serves the purpose of the ruling class.
Race is more accurately understood as
An anthropologic term. Its colloquial
Use is really a political function.
The political concept of race is a
Smoke screen to justify the disparity
In the quality of life forced upon
Misfortunates. I.Q. research reveals
Humaneness is not monopolized by skin tone.
This skin thin awareness of humanity
Is perpetuated as what is, when ignorance
Is what is the status quo.

A.K.A. THE HAWK

Old Jack Frost who is the boss is on his J O B
He gets his jollies raining ice follies.
Spreading sleet upon the ground, he jumps you
When you're down. Wind and snow at his command
Are not his only blow. Delights his mind to
See mankind lie helpless in the snow. Frost
Is cold, ice is bold, mean is mean as mean can be,
When old Jack Frost is on his J O B
Jack Frost is kicking boss for a man named
Simon LeGree. Jack Frost the kicking boss doth
Live in my home town. Keeps you in your snow
Bound place with his icy kind of frown. Takes
A guy who's down on luck an whisk away his only
Buck. Freezes him to concession pay, ups the
Price on each frozen day. With bills going up,
And luck going down, Jack no longer has a frown.
Then, with a blustery kind of smile he drags
His victims their last mile. Jack Frost the
Kicking boss is on his J O B. Colder times
Have not been known in all of hiss-tory.
Take for instance how Jack Frost doth treat
The lost. Spins them around, blows them down,
Gives place in which to drown. No colder clime
To drag a race to keep them in their casted place.
When Icy mold can't break the soul,
When slave to worker, to soldier to
Robotic, you just can't be, the Hawk
Will drown you in domestic flack.
Place unemployment monkey on your back.
With welfare on an epidemic flight,
Casting evil tendrils to all in sight,
Unemployment is so high,
Not one job left except our guy.
OLD JACK FROST IS ON HIS J O B

SEARCHIN

I'm Searchin Searchin Searchin
Everywhere I go
Searchin Searchin Searchin
For someone who wants to know
Seeking for the Searchers
Looking for the lost
Willing to guide the guilty
To the sin forgiving cross
All my waking moments
In pursuit
Of the God seeking lost
Wanting just to harvest

AMIGO QUINTERO

Hey brother, have you heard any truth lately?
Tell me tell me, I want to know.
Nothing seems real any more.
Have you heard any truth lately?
Can you point a word of right direction
To the New World Way?
I'm tired of sceneing
Just to fill a lonely day.
Truth is what I'm after
Got no time to trip another day.
This Land of Milk and Honey
Tough place to be without money.
Truth is what I pray to share
I want to find myself in The Father's care
I have no more time to jive or play.
Immigration is coming my way.
I want to go back home carrying the news,
The no more deportation blues.
It takes the truth to set man free.
Jesus is the way of life that guides
Man through this devil's strife.
His commands and words do say,
Remember! Keep The Seventh day.

HOLY THINE

Straight from the mercy seat
Words to save the lost from hades' heat
Light to spark your darkened soul
A guide within your very hold
Faster than the speed of thought
His will is set in place
Hold on to your shaken faith
He covers sin with boundless grace
Praise the Lord and praise His Will
He loves us all and always will
Coming from the pages of time
He calls to end the joker's rhyme
He that is filthy be filthy still
With all your effort you would not hear
In lustful living you find your cheer
Behold I come quickly
And My reward is just
Prepare to spend eternity
In whom you trust

IN THE CASE AGAINST FASHION

Fashion proves to be inspiration from without
How can woman perched high upon spiked heels
Know the Simplicity of her soul,
Should be Styled to reflect A Designer's will?
To walk in fashion's way causes others to see us
From a Wall Street point of view.
Seems to lead us astray, forgetting who gave
Us arches and placed our feet upon the ground.
Wall Street has a thing known as fashion. It
Causes women to go walking with a sway.
In the case against fashion it's of another day.
Nation time was for Dashiki, braided down
The fashion of the day.
Call my name of the motherland,
Show me light from the darker way.
Let me be brother to my sister as we sing
To celebrate our new found liberty.
In the case against materialism
Every freedom ain't free. Materialism dictates
Fashion, fashion dictates who we think we see.
Blocking out the light that shines from eternity.

IN THE MARKETPLACE OF MUSE

In the marketplace of muse
There are only so many thoughts
From which we have to choose.
All of life is a one act play
You really live in the time of
Yesterday.
Julius Caesar, Irving Schultz
Exchanging scenes today.
All of life is a one act play.
Doing its final act can be found
In yesterday.
An eye for tomorrow; the gift
Of prophecy.
Visions that come from on high
Seem confusing to the naked eye.
History; as understood by God,
Lets you know iron won't mix
With clay.
Concerns that spring upon us
Are of another day.
From the third and fourth generation
All unfolding to make prophecy true.
Men's hearts failing them for fears
Of the dawning new world day.
The time that Shakespeare
Wrote a dagger into Brutus' hand
Does coincide with all of life
Played out one more time again.

Choose the scene and choose it well.
There is only one generation
In all the time of man.
Be among the first to know
The voice that calls from within
To know the Fatherhood of God,
And the brotherhood of men.
In the marketplace of muse
There are only so many thoughts,
From which we have to choose.
Which ideas bare what kind of fruit?
A question to be asked by all thinkers.
Thinking, A Mind Must.
As sure as to breathe, Thinking
The thoughts of life.
In The Marketplace of Muse
What you mull is what you choose.
What you choose is what you get.
So get your choice together.
Choose The Father's Choice

"To everything there is a season, and a time
To every purpose under heaven. The thing that
Has been, it is that which shall be. And that
Which is done is that which shall be done: And
There is no new thing under the sun." Ecc. 3:1, 15

FREDERICK DOUGLASS

My name is Fredrick Bailey Douglass. I was Born a slave. In 1817, 1818 or 1819. I don't Really know when I was born, who my father was, And only saw my mother a few times. But one Thing I do know, it was planned ignorance of Who we are and laws to keep us that way. I Broke the law and taught myself to read and Write. At about twenty one I put on a sailor Suit, wrote myself a pass, and boarded a train For New York City. Once free, I joined the Abolitionist movement, working to establish The underground railroad. After many uprisings; Civil War and the spread of the abolitionist Movement, physical bondage was ended as the Law of the land. Alcohol, Dope and Ignorance Are the tools of slavery. They still destroy Millions. As it was yesterday, so shall it be Today, unless as a people we form the new Underground Railroad to Enlightment.
We need a people who recognize the tools Of slavers and will work as guides to their

Brothers. Conductors who care for their
Brothers, and are not ignorant of the times.
The past is repeated when you don't know
Who you are. Ignorance of who you are is
The lock on the chain of slavery. Ignorance
Of who you are IS the lock on the chain of
Slavery.

This speech was written as part of a stage
Play. As Mister Douglass, I was to appeal
To today's enslaved.

THOUGHTS OF A RUNAWAY SLAVE

Stealing my way to freedom
To escape, death I cannot fear.
Sleep under stacks of piled high hay
Stay out of sight in light of day.
Stalk Stalk the night away.
Circuitous is the trail
To leave the white man's hell.
In my berth upon this train
Sleep not in the meadow
Nor near the lane.
With the North Star as my beacon
I know I shall not fail.
To walk as free man in the light
Courage I'll need to face the knight.
Moss grows on the north side of a tree.
The more acorns and squirrels I see
The farther north I'll be.
Logs will float me across stream
Keep on the run to arrive at my dream.
North to freedom across the great divide.
Midway deep in Canada before
I break my stride.

STEAL AWAY

Struggling the road to freedom
A tune becomes my guide.
Directions The Father gave
Before I took my first stride.
Bouncing upon my father's knee
I learned the song he sang to me.
Jesus loves thee this we know
Up above the stars say so.
See the dipper in the sky
There's a North Star hanging nigh.
North is the route where free men abide
Heaven's gate they open wide.
Yes Jesus Loves Me
Yes Jesus Loves Me
Yes Jesus Loves Me
The heavens tell me so.

OPEN LETTER TO THE PRESIDENT

My name is A. T.

This is a letter drafted by one of the people of the delegation from Detroit. It is addressed to President Reagan, The White House, Washington, D.C. "Speak with the mike, sir." This is a letter drafted by an individual from the Detroit delegation. It is addressed to the President and we want to share it with you in the hope that it will inspire you to share your own thoughts with the President and others, we came to lobby.

Dear Mr. President:

We the residents of the Edward J. Jefferies home for public housing of Detroit, Michigan wish to take a few minutes of your time to express our concerns. All the residents of public housing dwellings are on a limited income, and if the conditions change financially we would not be able to live the level of dignity which was the main idea of the 1880 public housing act. We can not pay higher rent rates. We do not just ask this request for the rest of Detroit public housing, but we ask on behalf of public housing residents nationwide. Please, Mr. President, give this your careful prayerful attention. Hoping that you will grant this request.

—*Genieva Clerk*

* * *

Now that I am at this mike, I'm going to take a little more time to share some of my times from the '60s. I was standing at the mike that Bobby Kennedy was trying to get to when he was shot. That moved me to know the people who are our leaders are in danger. If you're wondering where all our leaders are, they're somewhere being afraid people. Because when you stand up and speak up for the poor; as you recall Martin Luther King was at the point of organizing the poor to have more say so in government. So we who are poor and have been subjected to the policies of this government and kept in a state of poverty must hold on to that dream Martin left with us so that we can accomplish the needs of the people. And I want you to know that if you organize and support the tenants' movement that we will succeed. That we will get the people who are in office to do a 180° turn from being supporters of Ronald Reagan to being supporters of the needs of the people. People, if you'll look in the word, you'll see the word says "Where there is no vision, the People perish." We have blind leaders at the helm. They have no vision. We need people who can have faith and confidence in doing something other than fearing Russia. We don't have to fear the Russians. It's not the Russians who are taking the food off our table, it's not the Russians who are running us out of our houses. It's the Reagan Administration. I know if this was a ku klux klan meeting, I'd be able to call a spade a spade. Well, I want to call evil evil. We have spiritual wickedness in high places. And unless we that believe in the powers that be that are greater than the federal government ban together this spiritual wickedness will crush us. But if we will have the confidence to stand on those things you be getting on Sunday morning when the preacher says, "Trust in the Lord." Stand up and Speak Your Piece and tell the people that you are free cause The Lord set you free. That you are gonna eat because The Lord supplies food for you. Then you will accomplish something. When you speak your piece in the name of a creator who created you to be free, then you can believe that these people in the Reagan Administration who work to destroy the welfare of the people will do an about face. Because they are only there because The Lord put 'um there. And when you stand up and say my God doesn't want you to treat me like this, they gonna have to change.

MICHIGAN MY MICHIGAN

Michigan Michigan
Profit is the business plan
In Michigan my Michigan.
Say Yes to Michigan.
Anything you want when you
Bring bucks to Michigan.
Come on up this very year
Spend that cash without any fear.
Wages are down and profits are up.
Workers drink from concessions cup.
Folk up here do what the bosses say
Kept in place by concession pay.
Business is as business does.
People guided by an overtime fuzz.
Michigan my Michigan
Say Yes to Michigan
Come say yes to yester-daze
View our land called Utopia Maze.
Blacks over here, Jews over there,
Poles in between.
When darkies choose not to live
Our ways.
We drive them back to Yester-daze.
Dearborn is our very own place.
Keeps the workers in their race.
Snow and ice wind and rain
Prove not to be the Black Man's gain.
Jim Crow is down where there is sun,
Now many of our Blacks are on the run.

Our darkies are quartered by overseer man,
And occupy the inner land.
Come on up to Michigan my Michigan
Robotics, Blacks would not be,
We could not drive them to the sea.
Wars don't end them from the land.
Now in Michigan my Michigan
Robotics are the master plan.
Come on up to Michigan
The South has risen again
Up North.

A. T. MUSING

SUB URBANITES

How some of these I don't like Detroit
People behave when they come into the city.
Reminds me of antebellum days.
Peons with mammies!
Sucking for all they can hold in fat
Greedy stomachs. Then getting up and
Pissing on their mammy.
Ungrateful. Undisciplined spoiled brats.
Offspring of the slave masters.

NEW FEDERALISM

How I loves ya
How I loves ya
My dear old massa
I'd give the world to be
In D-I-X-I-E
We loves you
Our dear ole Ronnie
Take us back to Dixie Land
Where each has his place
An mass's de man
No moe union dues I has to pay
No unemployment lines for T R A
Overseer man will have no play
Works us workers
'Til de work is done
We works on past de settin sun
Back to the good ole days
When massa was massa
And cared for his clan
Full employment for every hand
Children with chores
No idle time to play
Are the dreams I have of yesterday
Women's work is never done
Winches they be with the settin sun
When good ole daze return to the land
We tote dat barge and lift dat bale
Works for the massa to stay out of jail

No more food stamp fraud or welfare scam
We gets de chittlins, massa gets de ham
Back to de good ole daze
When winches filled de massa's lays
Life sure fits de mass's design
Use me til I has no mind
Makes me happy ta be dis way
He does me thinking
Tells me when to pray
The New Federalism
Is the old South scam
We return to the time
When they don't give a damn

OLD MAN BAND WAGON

Old man band wagon
Is old man greedy
He don't like people
And won't help the needy
He just keeps sucking along
Down with restrictions
Up with afflictions
Cut back here cut back there
No more low class medicare
Down with the down
Up with the up
Greed destroys incentives cup
Old man greedy
Just keeps sucking along
No more food stamps
No more summer camps
On things that do good
Greed has put a hood
Who needs fresh air?
Not if saving trees is gonna help
Seedy and his boys
Want to strip mine the forest
Ya know
Old man greedy
Just keeps sucking along
What a way to go
Got us livin without dough
"Let um eat cheese,"
Stock man is heard to say,
"We got so much its in ships
Just floating in the bay."
"Why should they be happy?"
Bonzo is heard to bark
Force them back to yesteryear
Let's keep them in the dark
Old man greedy budgets to the seedy
He just keeps sucking along

ONE BLOOD

He is your brother
Thou he doesn't know it
Beneath his skin
His blood will show it
Another's language
Through which to see
Keeps us apart
And from knowing we
I speak a tongue
That isn't me
Which says,
"I came down from a tree."
Lies and lies to hold us back
"He's not a brother,
His skin is black."
Never tells us what is true
From a single fount
Our blood was drew
Your skin is white
But with blackened heart
From the Father's rules
You choose to part
Deny the truth
Make God a lie
His word will out
By and by
Brotherhood
Is the way to be
Don't believe
That lie about a tree

RECONSTRUCTION

A war settled
each man as free
Ignorant bigots
won't let it be
Old Glory waves
land of the brave
Home of the free
to see a black
Eye to eye
does not agree
In massa's slavetime
philosophy
It takes one
to know one
I guess
it must be
They
did come down
From a tree

THEY,
THE ENDANGERED SPECIES

When toubob land would not let go
We swung in trees to and fro
The sort of man they bade us be
Drop the eye   bend the knee
Kiss my past
Hail ole England as the last
When toubob land would not let go
The black man's dignity would not
Take low
We swung in trees all over this land
Dipped in tar   drowned in sand
We paid our price to live life free
Old time times just can not be
We know the role we had to play
That part is part of yesterday
Up come a crop of ole daze fools
Wish us to live them by dem daze rules
In a southern breeze swung to and fro
Strange fruit doth wave
Making black blood flow
Scam that says you can't be you
Keep your eyes to the morning dew
Men engaged face to face
Eyes flash I hate your race
White only signs at blacks do blare
Jim Crow is spoken every where
For a black they just don't care
Denied the right to keep our land

An all out effort to break the black man
Impish children are heard to cuss
Take a seat at the back of the bus
Last hired   first fired
Raped by courts and hooded klan
Never satisfied that black is man
Forever in the ways of Cain
Slay your brother in the lane
No more strange fruit
Will we be
The southern breeze
Has blown its blow
Return to yesterday
We will not go
Been thru times
That makes me this way
I've seen the last of yesterday.

GOD'S BOUQUET

Red
black
brown
yellow
God's bouquet
chosen fellow
Who we be
is
who they not
What they get
is
what they got
Molded world
in decay
What a price
they have to pay
Raise your knowing
to the top
Review instructions
from our pop
Read the word
to scope his view
Thru his eyes
the truth is knew
Father Daddy
Grandpa Pop
He looks
down from the top

Back in time
The light has shown
In these times
It can be known
They
Pay the price
Who make men slaves
Down the tube
To Christless graves
Decayed life
On which to dine
Last day's meal
Bar B Q swine
Mango's
Aloes
Watermelon vine
Manna
Manjana
For those
Who are mine

A. T. MUSINGS

Where there is no vision the people are blind
Blind people are at the mercy of the sighted.
Mean one eyed forked tongue G. M. executive type
    overseers
Try to lead the blind astray.
The governoring monster says "What's good for
    America is
For one class to pig out on another."
G. M. founded on slavery as the law of the land.
How the west was won?
Thievery by lies, beads and trinkets for land and gold.
Deceit to control, unwilling to follow golden rule.
Aryan philosophy taught
Keep slaves ignorant, whatever you do don't let them
    read
In G. M. country Jim Crow ruled the roost when the
    plans
For the Doltville workers were laid. Automated
    regulated
Animated dolts. Dolts don't read, dolts owe their soul
To the company store, Massa does the thinking for
    his dolts.
One land of true grit
Led by dolts, a new standard in low,
A western way to go.
Dolts misled by massagement, unleaders, decadent
    hypocrites,
Who steal from the poor then blame the poor for
    poverty.
Leaders who have vision promote literacy.
All men need to read God's word, once one knows,
    there is
No return to domination by governoring monster.
Down with slavery Up with literacy

NOBODY KNOWS

Nobody knows the trouble I've seen
Nobody knows but Jesus
Nobody knows not even the white man
As I sing this song he still won't know
Stupid is as stupid does let's listen to him blow,
"I think I'll rule the world and make a slave of man."
All the rest of hiss-tory completes a dastardly plan
War and greed make up his time
That's filled with dirty deed, constantly behaving as
thou
The lie is true "God is not,
Neither is He a Jew
Others are inferior, ours to do it to."
Man that enslaves man needs a lie upon which to
stand.
How wrong a selfish being can be,
Forever plays the fool, knows no golden rule.
Affirmative action is not his favorite goal,
For yellow metal he'd sell his brother's soul.
When love of money denies me my honey
Something has got to go and it's not going to be my
dough.
I've been in the grip and squeezed beyond belief
Affirmative action a promise to bring relief.
From dawn to setting sun overseers crack the whip
To get me on the go and keep me on the run
But, I've worked to build a family dream
That truly sets me free
Live within the law of love

To keep the wolf at bay
Today he comes to set me back
But this is not his day
All my mind belongs to me and I'm not here to play
Steal from me
For all your gain
Life's not designed that way.
For thou you grow to rule the world
Your soul has seen its day.
He promised to come,
And Jesus is on his way.
Nobody knows the trouble I've seen or that which
Whitey's due.

WHY WHITE PEOPLE LIKE TARZAN

Tarzan movies are the outgrowth of books and comics. When first presented to the world, the Zeitgeist was one of no television and limited radio. The sordid past of slave masters had been replaced with the adventuresome dream of the opulent "gay" nineties. At this point in history, the American white man was exploring all points of the globe for "investment" purposes. With the industrial revolution came expansionist business holdings world wide. By the 1920s, the children of the nuevo rich were in need of stories about how their dads came to be the defenders of the world. Americans were still functioning with Jim Crow as the policy of the land. Therefore, Edgar Rice Burroughs felt safe and free to believe the politics and philosophy that made up the tenor of his times.

Paternalism was the natural outgrowth of superior inferior type of evolutionary thinking used to justify the policy and practice of Jim Crow America. Blacks as innately inferior in need of white culture and science and technology. Straight from the trees. Ignorant, unable to be civilized without contact from whites. They like it because it makes them feel superior.

REUBEN REUBEN

Reuben Reuben
I've been thinking
What a strange world
This would be
If the whites
Were all transported
Three degrees beyond
The northern sea
Clyde Clyde
I must say
Your up time musing
Sees a peculiar day
For how can life
Be what it is
Without the spark
To make it fizz
We need the whites
They let us know
There is a way
We should not go
In the sun
Where fun is free
Those who love
Look like me

WITHOUT REPENTENCE

The world without white men
A heavenly place to be
Indians and animals that long
Since cease to be
Abound in tune with nature
As the black man is finally free
Pure water—fresh air—sunshine
By which to see the fatherhood of God
Makes a brotherhood of we
A world without white men
To foul up history
Brotherhood is creed
Creation a fatherhood deed
The way of Cain accepts no blame
And lies to cover shame
He was his brother's keeper
Tho he slay him like he's game
Now without repentence
He's doomed on judgment day
A world without greed
Is how I hoped life could be
Long as Cain remains the same
No more whites need take his name

SELF DISCIPLINE

Self discipline
Is doing within
When outside
You're doing without

See your way out

YOKED

I ain't in no hurry
I have a long way to go
I'm in no hurry moving with the flow
A slowed haste is his yoked pace
Walking by his will is living in the flow
Keeping on life's path seekers get to know
Ask it shall be given: seek and ye shall find
Direct your thought to Him, hook up your mind.
I don't have to worry, neither shall I sweat
In all that's due an coming to me I know my need is met
Come what may I have hope in each day
For He shall direct my steps
I trust in Him: forgetting all my fears
He is through time in all our years

YOKE OF CAESAR

Every man can be king
If he'll seek the lower way
Every man can be king
With his heart set free
Today
Take Jesus as your leader
And the yoke of Caesar
Goes away

SOME OF MY BEST FRIENDS ARE POETS

Poets with their rhythm
Show the misery of man.
How they got that way
Strayed from the Father's
plan.
Poets tell it like it is
When few others can.
Shedding light upon the mind
To the wayward faring man.
The corridors of time
Are filled with same ideas.
Broken glass is everywhere
Life is a bloody scene.
Death still claims
The citizens of God.
Caesar still reigns as queen.
Everything that comes around
Goes.
In the time of life we're livin in
On Daniel's statue it's the toes.

Toubob land toubob land
A wicked ugly mess.
Filled with bloodshot eyes
And greedy gluttonous.
High of western lowliness.
Bright lights and promises.
Trademark of the cloven tongued
Toubob.
Fills his cup of iniquity,
Opulent in his last day glee
Check him out in prophecy.

IDEAS

Everybody has ideas
Ideas ideas ideas
Whose is the idea
I should follow?
You do what I say.
No!
I'll say what you do.
My ideas are as good as yours.
That's your idea about my idea.
Well I think . . .
Didn't I say I'd think for you?
I think I should think for me.
I said I don't mind thinking for you,
But you're too dense
To know what's good for you.
So to end the frustration
Of seeing you do something
Other than what I think you should,
I quit thinking for you.
You're on your own.
I've been trying
To tell you all the time
I can do my own thinking, thank you.
I think you need
To check your ideas
On wanting to think
For others.
You don't want to die

For others.
The idea
I find most interesting
To muse,
Concerns my possibly
Being able to live forever.
I'm not trying to think
For you brother, but
Muse on this
John Three Sixteen.

EVEN SO

Life is filled with
Who knows what.
The times we face
Looks bleek as smut.
Ups and downs
Ins and outs,
Quiet thought
Disturbing shouts,
Peaceful praise
Belligerent pouts,
Turned on-bombed out.
Even so
The future we face
Is ours to know.
Revealed by his prophets
His word says so.
Amos 3:7

SEASONAL FUN CLUB

Hi Luc,
Listened intently to you,
Loved you, till the fight went down.
What a beautiful servant of the most high.
Altogether apple of Jehovah's eye.
Doubting Thomas is what they called me;
Wanting just to do the things you do.
I did love him as the favorite, and would
That I could serve him close like you.
What a falling star would be like,
I never really really knew. How could I
Imagine what only you would do?

I'm so sorry you could not see the
error of your way. All the joy of heaven
Left us as you took man in your sway.
I had longed to do what you do, so I hoped
You'd receive him when he came to show the
Way. Surely, as Eve stood there; a reflection
Of the image that could be you or me,
Tempting her proved to be the wounding of
your head. He had promised a redeemer even
To the creator of the lie.
Prophet after prophet
Each living God's will
Calling for repentance
Even up Golgotha's hill
Salvation is God's promise
To believers in his son
What have you to say now
Oh whisperer
Since man has seen
The pages of time?

NO DOUBT NO FEAR

Living in a world of fear
Never knowing if you're really here.
Checking all the doubts of man.
Living catch as can,
And maybe if, double minded
On a quickened pace.
Wondering if you're being lapped
In the race of race.
Who can know,
When change is the only constant?
"Rely on tested ways that hold up
Over time." All who came before
Went this way, is the priestly
Kind of rhyme. "Come go the path
Of a thousand generations my son."
Father ancestor is heard to say.
"Tradition teaches a grooved path,
One on which your ancestors walked.
Good enough for granny is an offer
You can't refuse."
The mark of tradition is the sign
Of a man. Six sixty six is his number
And refuse it you can.
Flim flam, a polite way
To give back to the fathers
The groove that marks you image.
Father flim flam
Came along in 321 A.D.

A king of divine unction
Thought he.
The empty potentate
With a brew to lead the elect away.
Substitute God's holy day
And give them something
They can see and feel
With which to pray.
Flim told loud enough
Hidden by the pages of time,
Becomes flam. Sunday is a
Flim flam day, and never kept
By his chosen who point the way.
Ezekiel 20:20 is where I read it say
Those who are his children
Keep his special day.
How come some still live in doubt,
Not knowing what life's all about?
Finding reason to live in fear
Denying his spirit is always near
Not willing to read
The signs
Of tall tale flam,
America no longer
Behaves as a lamb.
Take the scales
From our eyes
That keep us from knowing
The devil's lies.
What time is it?
What must we be about?
Live by faith
Diminish doubt.
His word as guide
To teach us his will,
We've now over come
The potentates' spill.
Living through

The depths of flam
Now we rise
As the maker's lamb.
Another's voice we will not follow
Live our lives from an inside hallow.
Quiet for the calm of man
Should only be broken
To praise his plan.

HERE IS WISDOM

In Latin I learned the alphabet
Can be equated to numbers.

In the Bible I learned
Revelation 13:18 reveals
The Antichrist can be
Known by the title he
Is known by.

V	=	5
I		1
C		100
A		0
R		0
I		1
U		5
S		0
F	=	0
I		1
L		50
I		1
I		1
D	=	500
E		0
I		1
		666

RIGHTS

I got rights
You got rights
All God's children
Got rights
When you
Get your rights
Right
Everything
Will
Be righteous
Right
Everybody
Talking right
Ain't doing
Right
Right
Right
Gonna talk
Right.

LOVE IN THE LIBRARY

I take my love to the library, a joy we
Share together along life's quizzical way.
Tripping in different worlds
Taking time to play.
I love my love quietly near
With the Taj Mahal passing by.
Paris in the spring
New York on the Fourth of July.
Together in the library
A love light fills my eye.
All the world of man
Script upon the page.
Dreams reveal
A screen upon my mind
And a latent budding sage.
Tales of ancient cities
Told from a collective
Point of view.
Tradition is set aside
To be led by the inner you.
My thoughts
In the streets of Babylon.
Lovers in her garden muse,
"Our age shall never die."
Treat all men as brothers
To do other is the lie.
Bondage of one's fellows
Brings down the kingdom

By and by.
Love in the library
Is the way light came to me.
Knowledge of my brother
Seemed to set me free.
Love in the library
A place
For the blinded to see.
Your tender touch
In the Parthenon
Brings thoughts of life
As upon Socrates
Do we gaze.
"The unexamined life
Is not worth living"
The teacher is heard to say.
Check it out for your self
Is heard another day.
Rome as she is falling
Is not a pleasant place to be.
Raise our voices together
To deny slavery.
Hold on to righteous living
As the crown changes to see.
Living life together
In its renaissance
Awakens me and thee.
Tradition blocks out knowing
With approval of
The all fallible see.
Time changes
Problems stay the same.
Columbus sets to sea.
A place to practice slavery,
We call it home of the brave
Land of the free.
Free to do just as we please
No brotherhood shall be.
Tie men to chains

Kill them
If they won't be chattel
Dump um in the sea.
Never let him
Look you in the eye.
Break him from his knowledge
Feed him from the sty.
Lead his life in squalor
Looking for forty acres
A mule and pie in the sky.
I found love in the library
As I take a look at me.
Truth is where you find it
But reading allows you to see.
Found love in the library
Seen on the pages of time.
God blesses his children
Gives them rhythm
Gives them rhyme.

WOLF IN SHEEP'S CLOTHING

Whom do these people be?
They tell us where to aim our pee.
The seed within a gift from God.
To sow,
A choice one dare not trod.
So live thy style within his will
Plant your seed in the furrowed hill
Forget not the bird and the beetle too
Receive their share in the morning dew.
There is many a seed in a bearing pod
Who's way of existence is up to God.
How can I know if you should bare?
Life in a pod is what we share.
Some who know not your abode
Tell you how to carry your load.
I suspect tis just not true
That they would know what you should do.
Designed within life's natural flow
A woman's choice and she should know.
Seed thou sown won't always grow.
Take into mind the lurking crow
And beetles perched down below.
I may think you're seed for crow
God's real intent I just don't know.
Planted in the furrowed ground
Growth is sure health is sound.
Sometimes it's hard for thee to see
Thou pod we share not a common destiny.

Thou mounded dirt is where I be
There is not enough on top of me.
The heat of day doth dry me out.
While time below doth make thee stout.
I grow too fast to come to bloom
But faith doth keep me right in tune.
All is well that ends that way
Come back to serve another day.
Fodder is my fate to be
They turn the soil I start a tree.
The stout hearted pea is a loaf of bread.
Both our fates lay in his stead.
Seems like God knows what to do
Who's life is light who's life is stew.
Behold the 'lamb' who speaks of peace
Beneath the fur is ravenous beast.
He doth tell soft spoken lie
His real intent is buy the bye.
Just how did he behave in times of old?
Slavery set into motion by parsons gold.
Deny a race as God's creation.
Place on black backs the weight of a nation.
Tote that barge
Lift that bale
Just one glee happy
And you land in jail.
I don't believe
That she should be
A pawn in such hypocrisy.
She has the choice
To bare a seed,
Given by him
Who knows no greed.
What she must
Is up to her.
Let's call this beast
By its hidden fur.
A wolf

In sheep's clothing
Is who you be.
Trying to control
By liturgy
Learn to live
With all as free.

LE ROY

Send me my artist
Brush in hand
Pictures of light
As only they can.
Deep inside
A truth he has placed
Pictures of him
Leader of his race.
Help men to know
To trust in his will.
His love
For his children
Your stroke can reveal.
When troublous times
Descend on the land
He guides us through night
With the stroke of your hand.

RAISE THE PRAISE

Raise the praise
Michael is coming home.
Living life in a foreign land
Not always by the Father's plan.
Missing being the willing ark
Not guided by his inner spark.
Settled into midnight
Hustling darkness as the light.
Captured by desire
Intending right.
Calling out for freedom
Thou the darkness holds on tight.
Prayer for a prodigal
Remembered with the dawn
Though he revels far away?
Feeding with the swine
Brings pictures to the mind.
I'd be better off without my plan.
My father always led me
Beside still waters
Beneath the tree
Of love thy clan.
Break out the fatted calf.

BEYOND DEATH

One day we'll be living
With those who were dead
Alive again, rejoicing in stead.
United with those who've gone on before,
I know I'll love getting beyond death's door.
People who walked paths of clay,
Rejoice its family reunion day.
Brother Sister Mom and Dad
Kneel at the altar of Jesus' blood,
His spirit doth deliver in times of flood.
All are here to praise his name
Each generation declares the same.
We love him we love him we love him
Most dear.
Now is the time to invite him near.

GRANNY LOVE

Moving through the scenes of life,
    trying to find the real.
Reflecting back to Granny-Love;
    a match to the Father's will.

Light that lights the future coming
    from another day.
Granny-Love, the Father's choice to
    teach his child to pray.
Pray to God in Jesus' name to know
    his perfect way.
Follow in the steps of Christ,
    keep his holy day.

Jesus, our example in this fleshly temple,
Living out the scenes of life, Father,
    your will be done.
Shepherd to the little ones, guiding
    them through your love.

Keeping all through tender care,
    down as above.
Pick them up with Granny's arms
    and brush their wooly hair
Lead them to the path of light
    though Mama isn't there.

Tell them stories of salvation, of
    an old and God-sent way.
Jesus shines as the promised one
    redeeming the lost that stray.
Leading sheep through Granny-Love
    teach them they must pray.
Talk to God, a friend with ready ear,
    each and every day.

Granny-Love, Granny-Love, the ray that
    sees you through.
Given to the child in life to match
    it with his own.

Granny had the light of love in her eye
    whenever she looked my way.
Granny had the light in her eye that
    brought the joy of May.

Before she got religion, a tough Sister
    in her day.
That's why Mama had no time to sit
    with me and pray.

Granny found her love in God,
    living a new world way.
When I came along and just wanted
    to play.
Took us in like love was there to
    give away

Granny was the one God chose to show
    me how to pray.

    "Now I lay me down, your sheep,
    thank you for this day.
    Watch over Mama and Daddy.
    Bring us back to you in your
        will and way.
    Thank you for our Savior;
        in his name I pray."

Granny I'm glad you showed me, 'cause
    it's now the dawning of a new
    world day.
Some say it's Aquarius, others say
    Elijah is upon us.
But Granny knew the way.
Jesus live in Granny and to Him we
    always pray.

But for Granny-Love inside me,
    I'd surely have lost my way.
God bless all Grannies who have led
    His sheep the straight and narrow way.

We're in the time of harvest and Granny
    showed the way.
Here we come rejoicing, 'cause Granny
    showed the way.

—*A.T.*
*B.C. Love

ACORN

In the beginning
Was an acorn
That grew to become
A great tree
And from its branches
Hung a swing
That would hold
Five generations
Of a family.

Summers were never
Too hot
If you stood
In its vast shade
And in winter
You could see
The many nesting places
That the birds had made
Spring and Autumn
Brought with it
A certain special memory
What a grand ole oak tree
This acorn has become to me

"Unto you this day
A child was born . . .
And the child grew
And found favor
    with God and man . . .
This is my
Beloved son
In whom
I am
Well pleased. . . ."

Written especially for A. T. 12/23/78
by Joan Vassar Williams, a poet, artist and friend

ACORN II

I'm just a little acorn
That's what she says of me
Get what you sow
Be what you be
Sinking deep roots
To grow into a tree
Just a little acorn
Promise: A hope to be
Kind begats kind
The Father's word on sow
Being all the time
Keeping in the know
Just a little acorn
Growing in life's rhyme
Fruit in autumn
Seed in spring
Nut in the snow
Bloomin in the summer
The Father's way to grow
Sprouting with the dawn
Reaching for the sky
New growth every day
Time won't pass me by
An acorn in season
Is all I hope to be
An acorn in season
Surely is a tree
An acorn in season
Has lots of blessings
To be
Promise of a blessing
He liveth in thee

ACORN III

I'm just a little acorn
Bloomin right in time
Being what a nut
Is supposed to be
Laid back in the grass
Soaking up the sun
Here comes that squirrel
I wish I knew how to run

I'm just a little squirrel
Taking time to chew
Doing to a nut
What is long over due
Umm!

FRIEND II

I lost a friend today.
Life goes by so swiftly,
So little time to play.
In to our lives
Then they must go.
I lost my friend today,
Just part of a flow.
I tell myself these ways to see,
Still I know I know a space is left
At cease to be.
Memories: part that's left to know,
Are being made today
This space you've left
Has got to be filled.
I wonder if these roots
Are a good place to leave this acorn?

LIFE IS ONLY A DAY

Life is only a day
Yesterday is but a dream
There is no tomorrow
There is only today
So don't rush it away.

Life is what you make it
Death is how you take it
Love should be cherished
By all mankind
Hate should be left far behind
Cherish each day
As though it were your last
If bygones are cloudy
Forget the past.

Enjoy the earth surrounded by beauty
Kindness to all should be our duty
Lift up your heart and sing a song
For when your day is done, it will be gone.

Don't sit around, fret and frown
There is so much joy in our day to be found
Start your day with a hearty smile
This you'll always find worthwhile
Be kind to all
Regardless of poverty or wealth
And pray their troubles will end
And worries will melt.

Should God grant us another day
Let's start it off in the same gracious way.
Try to understand each person we meet
With a smile, a thank you, and a hearty greet
Try to lean just a little their way
Remember life is only a day.

Let's pray away
All the hate we hear and see,
From abroad and in our own backyard,
The land of the free.
Let's take all guns
And bombs and tuck them away,
For remember,
Life is only a day.

When you start your day
And you feel a little blue
A prayer will help,
Regardless what you do
Bend your knee
And bow your head
Remember, God isn't dead.

J. T.

To a person who bubbles with enthusiasm, interest, eagerness, activity, interest in others, and maybe this, too, will express something.

— D. Schwartz

A GAY SPIRIT

A gay spirit
Is like the sun
Peeping from behind the clouds,
Its radiance shining down
On sombered fields below.

A gay spirit
Is like the sunlight
Streaming thru the thick clouds
Above an overcast sea
Streaming with brilliance,
And somehow saying, "Again"

A gay spirit
Is like the trickling song
Of a brook moving thru
The sonorous fields,
Wild, silent, and stillness
Yet, now broken with the
Delightful song of life.

A gay spirit
Is to tired souls
Like the warm sun shining-thru
The shoals of clouds, dark overhead
And on the earth below
Radiance, and living
Spreading forth their cheer

And the truth that life
Is perpetually good,
No matter how rough, craggy, jutty,
Or painful the road may become.

A gay spirit
Fills those around it
With the proximity of its cheer
With the laughter of its heart,
And the hope of its soul,
Giving forth an abundance
Of needed love, mirth, joy,
Compassion, and the
Soul of living
To those lost in the
Darkness of their own
Inner words of conflicts, confusions,
Despairs,
And letting them see and feel
The glow of the spirit called 'life.'

ODE TO A COUNSELOR

Hey mellow! Check this out,
Know what you put me up on
        goodness
What reality is about.

Now my city is cold in winter
And brutal year round.
A city where the strong stand-up
While tricks keep falling down.

Now I been out there
Out there hanging tuff
No punk a– nigger could tell me
No sh– about any love

Know why? They scared,
Of those like me
Yet running sh– bout
How they cared so much
For our needs.

They approached me with caution
Looking both ways.
They crawled round to see me
With their bullsh– plays

I woulda been out here for life
Playing on them fools,

Who use good as a front
To make me think them cool

Then I met you and
You extended your hand.
The only difference was
You came on like a man.
In a sh– talking kind of way
You put me up on God and
Yet the nigger ain't no lame.

So I thought, well, must be
Something that he wants.
Money, reefer, connects to
A little cunt.
Then I re-cognized
You with dreams
Someone just like me
Able to cop alone what he wants
From the streets.

I saw a new ability
Even above my own,
And suddenly
I felt following you
Might lead me home
To the real me.

So I listened and listened
And listened some more.
Till I was five, ten, twenty
Miles from your door.
And I heard.

Suddenly! The street lights,
Shining thru my windows
Of my car,
Took on a glow of heaven
Like they were earthly stars.

From a distance I could hear
The meanings of your words
I felt good, I felt free
As the flight of soaring birds

I realized truly tuff ain't
Bout shi-.
Cause when it comes to good
Tuff cain't deal with it

Now my life can travel
Just about any where
Twelfth and Blaine to Church
And neither makes me scared

Now I can love and
Love in either place
Now I see with love fear
Really has no place

I hear your message mellow
Hear it loud and clear
Love and good together
Stop every inner fear.

—*R. Brown*

MY PEOPLE

My people, my people,
My beautiful black people.

I wish you could read
As well as you can dance;

I wish you could talk
As well as you can sing;

I wish you could walk
As well as you can run;

I wish you could pray
As well as you can swear;

My people; my people
My beautiful black people;

I wish you could love
As well as you can hate;

I wish you understood
As well as you misunderstood;

I wish your work was
Harder than you play;

I wish you would smile
As well as you frown;

I wish you would respect
As well as you disrespect;

I wish you would think
Better than you thought;

My people; my people;
My beautiful black people;

As well as you can't
I wish you could,
If you could,
I know you can.
My people; my people;
My beautiful black people.

—S. J. Stringer

THIS THING IS FROM ME

I have a message for thee today my child.
I will whisper it softly in thine ear,
In order that the storm clouds which appear
May be gilt with glory, and that the thorns
On which thou mayest have to walk, be blunted.

The message is but short—a tiny sentence,
But allow it to sink into the depths
Of thine heart. And be to thee as a cushion
On which to rest thy weary head.

This thing is from me

Hast thou never thought that all which
Concerns thee concerns me also?
He that toucheth thee, toucheth me,
Apple of mine eye.
Thou hast been precious in mine eyes,
That is why I take special interest in
Thine upbringing. When temptation assails thee,
And the "enemy comes in like a flood,"
I wish thee to know

This thing is from me

Hast thou made plans and then come ask me
To bless them? I wish to make thy plans for thee.
I will take the responsibility for it is too
Heavy for thee. Thou couldest not perform

It alone. Thou art but an instrument and not
An agent. Hast thou designed fervently
To do some great work for me? Instead
Of that thou hast been laid on one side
On a bed of sickness and suffering?

This thing is from me

I was unable to attract thy attention whilst
Thou wast so active. I wish to teach thee
Some of my deep lessons. It is only those
Who have learned to wait patiently, who can
Serve me. My greatest workers are sometimes
Those who are laid aside from active service
In order that they may learn to wield the
Weapon of prayer. Art thou suddenly called
To occupy a difficult position full of
Responsibilities? Go forward, counting on me.
I am the God of circumstances. Thou hast not
Been placed where thou art by chance, but
Because it is the place I have chosen for thee.
Didst thou not ask to become humble?
Behold I have placed thee in the very place
Where this lesson is to be learned. It is by
Thy surroundings and thy companions that the
Working of my will is to come about. Hast
Thou money difficulties? Is it hard to keep
Within thine income?

This thing is from me

For I am he that possesseth all things.
I wish thee to draw everything from me,
And that thou depend entirely upon me.
My riches are unlimitable. Put my promise to the
Proof so that it may not be said of thee,
Yet in this thing ye did not believe the Lord
Thy God! Art thou passing through a night
Of affliction?

This thing is from me

I am the man of sorrow and acquainted with grief.
I have left thee without human support that in
Turning to me thou mightest obtain eternal
Consolation. Has some friend disappointed thee?
One to whom thou hadest opened thine heart?

This thing is from me

I have allowed this disappointment that thou
Mightest learn that the best friend is Jesus.
I long to be thy confidant. Has someone said
False things about thee? Leave that and come
Close to me, under my wings away from the place
Of worldly dispute, for I will bring forth thy
Righteousness as the light, and thy judgment
As the noonday. Have thy plans been all upset?
Art thou crushed and weary?

This thing is from me

I am giving the position full of difficulties
For the reason that Jehovah thy God will bless
Thee in all thy works, and in all the business
Of thy hands. This day I place in thy hands
A pot of holy oil. Draw from it freely, my child,
That all circumstances arising along the pathway,
Each word that gives the pain, each manifestation
Of thy feebleness may be anointed with oil.
Remember interpretations are divine instructions.
The sting will go in the measure in which thou
Seest me in all things.

A VISION OF THE CROSS

My head tossed restlessly upon my pillow
While outside in the darkness the Thunder rolled;
Then, the lightning before the Thunder,
Within my head, there came a vision of horror untold;
I saw the Blood.

One brief moment of unbelievable anguish
Was stamped on my memory as the lightning flashed,
And lit up old Golgotha; three painful forms,
Crucified on Crosses were silhouetted against the
heavens.
Down the side of the center figure and flowing
Freely from the emaciated form,
I saw the Blood.

Mother Earth trembled like a reed in the wind, and
Huge boulders came tumbling down the shaking
mountains.
The fowls of the air disappeared into the dense
darkness,
And there followed an uneasy calm. But hark the
stillness
Is broken by a voice clear and musical
"Eloi Eloi Lamasabachthani." I looked again toward
The three crosses from whence came the voice,
I saw the Blood.

Oh precious Blood, Oh cleansing Blood, that
sanctified
Calvary, Flowed on and on and on and on until
It sanctified me.

—*Uncle Harry*

TODAY

Today is very special,
Just because it is today;
Not to be used regretting
Haunting deeds of yesterday.

Tomorrow is like a shadow,
Without a reality.
A shadow of things to come,
And wrapped in obscurity.

Today, then, was not given
We mortal men to borrow,
Worries or even problems
That just might come tomorrow.

You cannot live tomorrow,
Neither call back yesterday;
No one ever lived tomorrow
Until it became today.

This thought's therefore concluded,
You had better do today
All the good that you can do,
In a kind and loving way.

You'll reap that special blessing,
Of hearing the Master say,
This world's a little better, son
Because you have lived today.

—Uncle Harry

SMILE AND LOVE

Smile, it has value, but no cost,
Love, because love is never lost,
Both are worth more than purest gold,
They win young hearts and cheer the old.

Love is a winner, not gainless,
And a little smile is painless,
In combination, they are tops
They need no help, they need no props.

They're an antidote for sorrow,
Can even make a glad tomorrow
They have joy and they have gladness,
They banish gloom, strife and sadness.

Love cannot be bought, it's priceless,
And without it, life is useless,
Therefore, all men are great, whatever their race
When they let love take hatred's place.

—Uncle Harry

THE RISE AND FALL

The rise and fall of western civilization can be understood as one examines the central unit of the American populace. The nuclear family is the social unit that sets the tone for the quality of life lived by its members. In the United States the ethic has been to promote and respect this type of relationship. A husband, a wife and their children comprise this unit. When this unit functions as it should, the product is a healthy personality. Thus, a healthy country. For hundreds of years in this country a marriage carried the respect of government, church and individuals. However, since the industrialization of America, people have separated from their responsibilities in these units, and lead solitary, uninvolved lives. Working and living in cities has lessened the family dependence, further weakening the relationships. To quote a friend, "Cities are not made for children and other living things." Those life styles which do not base themselves on independent, responsible use of family assets are soon dependent on a system of government. While this welfare may have as its goal to aid, it really sets a trap. The needy are trapped into a dependent relationship which destroys responsible independence. Marriage was ordained for the purpose of peopling the earth and perpetuating the race. Marriage is also to promote social order and human happiness: to prevent irregular affection and through well-regulated families to transmit truth, purity and holiness from age to age.

In its ideal state, marriage is the key to restoring the

principles that lead to a healthy society. Respect begats respect and when colonization of fifty million blacks began, it could only succeed when there was wholesale destruction of the black family unit. For hundreds of years, the Victorian ethic of family respect was propagandized as the American way. The practice was to have a bed wench or concubines and utterly disrespect the black family ties. One may say all he wishes about how people should live their lives, but if all the time you are destroying others God-given rights, the reaping surely is what you have sown. Sow family destruction, reap it. Remember God is on the side of the fatherless.

KNOWING

Looking down on Babylon: One sees a play of time.
Scoping into yonder year; scene for scene in kind.
Cognize what has been, re-cognize when my line due.
All the world's a stage, I can't miss my cue.
Doing what's been done the hippest thing that's new.
Libations to the king of night; as darkness covers you.
Down fall the walls of Salem; and free man is turned slave.
No more living by God's will; a fate seen worse than grave.
But from the children of the Lord; Daniel stands up tall.
When the play is played to end; the end's no end at all.
Dreamer in a strange land; of a day yet to be.
Before the king to bring him light, times no time to me.
God know the end and beginning; speaks thru prophecy.
The play of time seen just once, gets you in the know.
Seventy weeks to Messiah; starting a week ago.
Now showing in Babylon: a seance and a trance.
A guile of life to bring man strife and kill
Your heaven sent chance. On stage the king's palace:
A dreamer's dream comes true before naked eyes
The craft of sin in full screen review
Scenes change and stay the same; a lion's in the game.

Daniel of the lion's den; visionary of his day
Chosen by the God of light in Babylon to pray.
Bowed before pagan gods the people kneel this day.
High upon the plane of Dura; image of the latter day
Babylon, Medo-Persia, Greece, Imperial Rome,
All on stage to play their part, yet it's not the end.
Up comes a dragon beast and proves he's no man's
friend.
For time and time and division of time
He takes the center stage. Set the children's teeth
On edge, playing his part in rage.
Babylon, the head of Gold, a nation gone astray.
Weaves a tale of false ideas; game for the latter day.
Five thirty eight B.C. an image rises tall
The dream of the king is the stuff of time
That shows the nation's fall.
Bow down to occult guile; the game that's played
thru time.
Kiss the king on his toe, let the stars guide you so.
Palmistry, a plan revealed to show tomorrow's path
Following the tricksters rap brings down the
Father's wrath
Unto two thousand days and hundreds by three
The close of time should be, but day unto day
Is given to thee.
The children of the Lord as slave
In a far off hateful land
Delivered from the wickedness set up by Aryan man.
Messiah comes to save the day
Proving iron won't mix with clay.
Ignorance plus ignorance
Is equal to its sum.
Living blind in Babylon
Is surely living dumb?
Set your mind on the word
To get it in the know
Follow in the ways of Christ he soon is due to show.

CLASSIFIED ADS FOR THE MIND

Avoid early enslavement
Learn to say your A B Cs

See right be right
See wrong go to hell

Reading brings light
To the mind

Blacks who read
Break the law
Of enslavement

Buyers and refiners of gold
Teachers of virgin minds

Visit your local library
Avoid early mind breakdown

Library visits immunize
Against dumbness

Evil men write lies
Weak men sell them
Helpless men diet on lies

Blacks who read break
The law of enslavement

Be well read
Avoid a void mind

Don't not keep the Sabbath
A double negative is a positive

Do not read trash
Avoid poison for the mind

Avoid doltism immunize
at
The local library

Escape boredom
Read a good book

Reading assures
Awareness

Support your local
Librarian
He needs it

S
 O
  A
   P
    S
R-4
Dopes

Foul language
Inhabits
Evil minds

Stamp out smut
Reading a sight
Right

New way out of
Poverty
Literacy = riches

Help found in
Words of life
Read the Bible

Ignorance is
Dangerous

Soaps rape
The mind

Beware
Illiterates
S
 L
  I
   P
    P
     I
      N
       G
Into darkness

See signs
up
Think

Laws against black
Literacy
Never repealed

Wanted: free thinkers
Readers rate

Avoid stupidity
Learn to read

Soaps equal
Food for fools

Fools remain blind
Wisemen read

Think
        up

TV = trash

Love thy librarian
Support literacy

Axiom: high ignorance
Equals easy enslavement

A truth: no money
No easy life

Wanted: Free thinkers
See pictures of the
Future: John the
Revelator

The better life available
Work—discipline—commitment
Lazy dummies need not apply

ABCDEFGHIJKLMNOPQRSTUVWXYZ

Soaps smart
                Same
                Old
                Ancient
                Practiced
                Shi-

Renaissance equals
New you

Reading relieves
Not knowing

Fools find fault
With their ABCs
Read: avoid foolishness

Support your local librarian
Return overdue books

Love your local
Librarian
PRN

Egyptologist needed
Lead people back across
The read: see

Free reading lessons
Call June Brown

Avoid early enslavement
Learn to say your ABCs

Resist enslavement
Reading writing and freedom

S
O
A
P
S
S
U
C
K

Stamp out mind blindness
Be well read

Books brighten

Learn to be well read
Know the truth it has
Been spelled out in
Thy sight

D
O
W
N
W
I
T
H
D
O
L
T
S

S
C
O
P
E
Y
O
U
R
F
U
N
K
And Wagnalls

To learn truth
It must be read
Nobody's speaking it

Teach black children
To read their freedom
Depends upon it

Celebrate Martin's day
Remember Paul Robeson

A. T. MUSINGS

Where two racists gather
To engage in friendly
Mutual benefit,
Jesus shall not be.

Right wing conservatives
Worship at the shrine
Tradition. No racist
Is a true Christian.
Tradition teaches racism.
Fundamentalists accept
Thus saith the Lord.
Racism is cancer of the soul.
Reagan's policies have
The effects expected
When racist repressive
Oppressive leaders
Bring back the old
Traditions.
Pious dogs
Killed Jesus.
It takes a racist
To promote racism.

HATES GLARE

Used to be
They glared at us
Then uttered
A plebian growl,
"Nigger."
Now with law that
Says we're equals,
Their look contains a smile.
Beneath this sophistry facade
A heart is filled with guile.
Smiling faces destroy races
Denying black as God's child.
Hate;
Contained in a look down attempt,
Makes they who have
This hate filled stare,
The no class whimp
Who just don't care.
Invisible people just ain't there
Is the meaning in a bigot's glare.
Look on past as though he isn't there.
Pat him on his head, what the heck.
Treat um with 'Benign neglect.'
Deny their men deserve respect
Hate is cancer of the soul.
Destroys the vessel
That gives it hold.
Look with hate
Upon whom you will.
The glare you give
Will its looker kill.

DEAR LITTLE ONE

Dear Little One,
I find it a joy to be once again sharing the milk of life with you. I know while you were at my bosom it was never in me to be mean to a red necked blue eyed baby-boy. I remember singing love songs to you as though you were mine. Even when I was told to feed you and no longer to suckle my own. Love begats love and as my contribution to future good race relations I dutifully filled you to overflow. Singing and sucking, Jesus love you this I know. Can a mother reject her own child? Can a child despise the being at whose nipple he's weaned? What a disappointment it has been to watch you grow up to carry on the traditions which gave you first choice. As I did my part I believed one day God would bring about justice. Now that you have continued in constructive engagement with injustice, I am writing you to let you know this is a losing proposition. You are weighed in the all seeing eye of God and found to be seed of the unrepentent. Yo mammie can no longer extend prayer in your behalf. May His justice come swift and soon.

— *Yo Mammie*

THE WOUND IS HEALED

The wound is healed
But nobody knows
The time of time
A statue's toes
The darkness returned
As in ancient days
The Middle Ages
Latest new craze
The wound is healed
And seems no one knows
The rock of ages
Breaks up the toes
An image stands
To ape the past
The truth when known
Will make you gasp
Back to the ways
Of used to be
Image of a beast
In the land of the free

TYJ

Last night I lay asleeping
I dreamed a dream so rare
Laid back in the hay
I really wasn't there
Upon my mind I saw it be
My voice heard in history
A chance to tell it like it is
No more lies from Father Wiz
Now I'm standing on a stage
All the ears are set for sage
The question comes to my mind
Can words fitly spoken
Bring sight to the blind
If all my brothers' freedom
Depended just on me
Can words fitly spoken
Make the blinded to see
Thank you Jesus for Your love
Via the Father's sight
We see this day as from above
Thank you Jesus You let us see
The real is who You made us be
In all the play that takes up time
A cross to bear for those who are thine
The underdog is who You choose
In olden days it was the Jews
Gentiles though we brothers be
Within our hearts we live for Thee

Toubob land put a lock on our mind
Destroyed knowledge of our ancient kind
Jesus stumbling on his way to die
Simon goes boldly up that hill
A brother carrying his cross carries it still
Cush and Nimrod had come to know
In tune with nature let life flow
Down through time it has reached this day
His children are the lowly and to him we pray
We are the children of the Lord
It's what the pages say
Chosen for the time of life
Known as the latter day
Lift the scales that blind the mind
Toubob tales say kind ain't kind
Life is made from a Father's plan
Each child is child each man is man
Those who fail to see by light
Sale their wares in dead of night
Down through time they made it be
Proclaimers of his word
Die of heresy

GLOSSARY

Muse-ition—Name chosen by A. T. that describes his style of writing.

Dung—Waste matter droped by animals, manure.

Papilion—A butterfly.

Massa—Slave master.

Massagement—Style of management which denies dignity of workers.

Imprint—Characters which indicate nature of creator.

'A muk'—Out of control.

Miller's wheel—The all seeing eye of God.

Family jewels—The sex organs.

Dit ah peer—Disappear.

Hiss-tory—Pseudo history, lies which represent the devil's way of interpreting time.

Mantra—A chant used to center oneself in meditation.

Tho-we—A way of spittin and rejecting an idea.

Oohzi—An automatic gun.

Snook—A lying bigot.

Antebellum—The time of physical slavery in America.

Jim Crow—Term used to describe policies and practices of segregation after the Civil War.

Dixie-crat—Southern politician dedicated segregationist.

Simon Legree—Slave master.

The Hawk—Jack Frost; a bitter cold wind.

Overtime fuzz—State of mind of Doltville workers.

T R A—Training reimbursement agreement.

Toubob—Word used by Africans to describe a foul smelling caucasoid whose purpose was to enslave Blacks.

G.M.—Governoring Monster, spirit of American Industrialist. Inventors of assembly line massagement.

Amigo—Friend. A word best embodied by Roberto.

Liturgy—Prescribed forms of public duty, enforced worship, i.e., blue laws.

Cain—Son of Adam. First murderer on this planet. Killed his brother because of differences in worshipping God.

Aryan—A member of 'prehistoric' people who spoke Indo-European. Caucasian gentile.

Palmistry—The occult practice of trying to read the past or future by interpreting the pattern of lines in the palms.

Gentiles—A non Hebrew, a non Mormon, a pagan, a clannish heathen.

Heresy—A belief not in agreement with the accepted traditions of the middle age church which, if maintained after being asked to recant, is punishable by death.

Mammie—Black woman chosen to breast feed the child of the slave master.

Flim Flam—To con, deceive with intent of robbery.

Zeitgeist—Aryan word for tenor of the times.

Lie about a tree—Darwin's theory of evolution interpreted by Aryan, WASP colonist as scientific fact, which was the rationale used to justify slavery.